A GOOD YEAR BOOK™

SCIENCE CHALLENGE

190
Fun and Creative
Brainteasers for Kids

LEVEL 1

D1021025

GOOD YEAR BOOKS

are available for most basic curriculum subjects plus many enrichment areas. For more Good Year Books, contact your local bookseller or educational dealer. For a complete catalog with information about other Good Year Books, please contact:

Good Year Books
P.O. Box 91858
Tucson, AZ 85752-1858
www.goodyearbooks.com

ISBN: 1-59647-067-4

1 2 3 4 5 6 7 8 9 10 - DR - 08 07 06 05

Illustrations: Tom James
Design: Daniel Miedaner

Neat!

Ashley and Jack are running through the sprinkler. Water drops are flying everywhere. "Look, a rainbow," Jack says to Ashley. What made the rainbow?

3

Light shining through water drops is refracted (separated) into colors in the same way as when light shines through a glass prism. The different colors of light that make up the white sunlight are bent by different amounts as they pass through the drops. This process separates the colors so you can see them.

Fact!

Air is all around us, even though we can't see it. Air takes up space. What is one way you could show that air takes up space?

4

Blow up a balloon or puff out your cheeks.

science challenge

Level 1

Listen!

Carlos says that drinking milk will give you muscles. Annie says Carlos already has muscles. Who is right?

5

Everyone is born with muscles, but a nutritious diet, including milk, helps keep your muscles strong.

Really?

Some insects called water striders can walk on water as easily as you walk on a sidewalk. How can they do this?

Water has a kind of skin, called surface tension, on which the water strider can walk.

6

Look!

Do most babies look like their parents? Not always. Some babies have to go through stages before they look like adults. What does a baby butterfly look like?

7

A baby butterfly is a caterpillar. Even tiny butterflies are adults.

science challenge

Level 1

Weird!

How many ways can you sense sounds? You can hear sound with your ears. You can feel sound too. How can you feel sound?

Place your ear on a table. Hit the table to make a sound. Feel the vibrations. Or turn up your stereo and feel the floor thump. (Don't do this for long!)

8

Look!

Last year, Mr. Brown had many dandelions in his yard. His neighbor, Mr. Green, had none. This spring, Mr. Green's yard has many dandelions. How did the dandelions get to Mr. Green's yard?

9

The wind carried the dandelion seeds from Mr. Brown's yard to Mr. Green's. Every summer and fall you can see dandelion seeds as their "parachutes" carry them on the wind.

Neat!

Light lets us see. Make a pinhole in the end of a closed shoe box. Peek through the pinhole. Can you see inside the box? What happens if you put a lighted flashlight in the box?

You cannot see inside the box without light. Once you put the flashlight inside, you can see.

Who Knew?

Some relatives of the dinosaurs are still living today. One has a very hard shell. Another has sharp teeth and powerful jaws. What are these dinosaur relatives?

11

Turtles; crocodiles and alligators

Listen!

If you drop an orange and a rubber ball from the same height, which will hit the floor sooner? What force makes things drop to earth?

They will both hit at the same time. Gravity, which is the pull of the earth, makes them fall.

12

Cool!

Mammals have fur and birds have feathers for protection. What covers butterflies and moths?

13

Butterflies and moths are covered with colored scales.

Weird!

Mike shows his friend a magic trick. He rubs a balloon on his head and then waves it over some bits of paper. What happens when he does this?

The balloon is charged with static electricity from Mike's hair. If it is a dry day, the paper will jump to the balloon.

14

Fact!

Insects form the largest group of living things on earth. Over 800,000 species have been identified, and there probably are many millions. How can you identify an insect?

I AM AN INSECT! Don't BUG ME!

15

Insects have six jointed legs, three body parts, and, usually, two pairs of wings.

Fact!

Insects have skeletons on the outside of their bodies called exoskeletons. What supports your body?

Your body is supported by a skeleton of bones inside (an endoskeleton).

16

Look!

If you put your hand in front of your face, you can feel your breath. When the air is cold, you can see your breath. What makes it possible to see your breath when it's cold?

17

The cold air causes the water in your breath to condense, forming a tiny cloud.

Level 1

science challenge

Weird!

If you took a spaceship to an alien planet, you would need three things to survive. What would you need?

18

Food, water, and air

Cool!

Make a parachute. Tie one piece of string to each corner of a handkerchief. Tie a weight at the ends of the strings. Toss the parachute into the air. Why doesn't it fall quickly?

19

Air pushes up against the parachute and slows it as gravity pulls it down.

Listen!

Sarah is showing her rock collection. Some rocks are very rough. Others are smooth. Jim says the smooth rocks came from a beach. How does he know this?

20

Most small stones are pieces that have broken off larger ones. These pieces are rough. The smooth stones were rolled back and forth in water, which ground off the rough surface.

Look!

An animal lives under the porch at Katie's house. It has two big, flat front teeth; small ears; and fur that is grayish-brown. Does this animal eat meat? What could the animal be?

No, if the animal were a meat-eater, it would have sharp, pointed teeth. This animal is probably a woodchuck (groundhog) or other rodent and eats grass and other plants.

Really?

Even though snakes have no legs or feet, they can swim and climb trees as well as animals with feet. Are snakes mammals or reptiles?

Snakes are reptiles.

22

Neat!

Soak a bean seed in water for a day. Then peel off the skin and open the seed. Look for the tiny sprout. A magnifying glass helps. How many parts does a bean seed have?

23

Bean seeds are dicots. There will be two distinct halves to the seed and two seed leaves. Most of what you see is food for the baby plant. With a magnifying glass you can see the tiny plant with its two seed leaves (cotyledons).

Who Knew?

How are a watchdog and a maple tree alike?

24

They both are protected by barks.

Cool!

Take two balloons, one blown up and one deflated, and tape one to each end of a ruler. Tie a string around the center of the ruler and pick up the ruler by the string. Which side is heavier? What does this show?

25

The blown-up balloon is heavier, showing air has weight.

Listen!

Daniel went to his brother's basketball game. He wanted his brother to hear his cheering. So he cupped his hands around his mouth. Will this really help?

26

Yes, it will. Sound travels in waves that spread out. By cupping his hands around his mouth, Daniel is concentrating the sound.

Weird!

Your tooth fell out! You put it under your pillow. In the morning you find a dollar and a note that says, "Drink three glasses of milk every day." Why is this good advice?

27

Milk has calcium. You need calcium for strong bones and healthy teeth.

Cool!

Rub your hands together. After a while you will probably feel heat. Why do your hands feel very warm after rubbing?

As you rub your hands together, you are creating friction. Friction happens anytime things rub together. Friction changes the motion energy of your hands to heat energy.

28

Really?

Fish live underwater, but they need to breathe oxygen just like you do. How do fish breathe?

29

Fish take in water through their mouths and pass it over their gills. Oxygen is dissolved in the water. The gills collect the oxygen from the water.

science challenge

Level 1

Listen!

Keesha and Sam want to move a large box. It's too big to carry or drag, but Keesha thinks of an easy way to move it. What would be an easy way to move the box?

30

Put the box on something that will roll. Rolling friction is much less than sliding friction.

Fact!

Energy is what makes things move or get warm. Have you heard of "burning energy" when you play? What does "burning energy" mean?

31

Burning energy means using up the energy you get from your food. You are burning energy when you move, talk, breathe, or even digest food.

Neat!

Stir salt into a cup of water. Tie one end of a string to a paper clip and the other end around a pen. Place the pen across the cup and let the paper clip hang in the water for a few days. What do you see on the string?

Salt crystals

Weird!

What is black and white and red all over? A zebra with a sunburn. How can the sun burn your skin?

33

The ultraviolet rays in sunlight burn your skin. Your eyes can't see the ultraviolet rays, but they are the most dangerous rays in sunlight.

Who Knew?

One of the oldest plants on earth is moss. You can find moss growing anywhere there is shade and moisture. How do scientists know moss is an old plant?

HOME OF
MR. P. MOSS

34

They have found fossils of mosses in very old rocks. Mosses have no true roots, stems, or leaves.

Listen!

Richard says that he is a red-blooded American. Tasha says that red blood has nothing to do with being an American. What gives blood its color?

Blood is red because of red blood cells. The red cells contain iron, which is red, and helps to carry oxygen from the lungs.

Look!

Kim asked her grandfather, "Why is the moon round tonight?" "The moon is always round," he said. "Sometimes we just can't see all of it." Why can't we always see all of the moon?

36

We see the moon because sunlight reflects off it. Sometimes, as the moon moves around the earth, the earth blocks some of the sunlight. Then the moon does not look round.

Fact!

Can sunlight heat water? Think of how you might find an answer to this question. Try your idea. What did you find out?

37

Yes, sunlight can heat water.

Really?

Dinosaurs lived millions of years ago. Many of them were very, very large. Were dinosaurs the biggest animals that have ever lived?

No. They may have been the biggest animals on land, but blue whales are the biggest animals that have ever lived. A blue whale can be 100 feet long and weigh 150 tons.

Fact!

Exercise, such as running and jumping, is good for you. How is running and jumping good for you?

Exercise keeps your muscles, joints, and other body systems in top shape. Exercise makes your heart muscles and lungs work harder, keeping them strong.

Cool!

Camels can store enough water in their bodies to last for several days. Why is it important for camels to be able to store water?

Camels are desert animals. Sometimes they must go for many days before they can find a drink.

Fact!

All living things can be grouped. Plants that have thick, woody stems and grow tall are grouped as trees. What group of animals have scales and fins and live in water?

41

They are fish.

Fact!

Wasps are insects that build their own homes. Wasp homes are called nests. The nests can be made of paper or mud. Are wasps and bees the same kind of insect?

No. They are both insects, but different species. Bees' nests are made of wax and contain combs that store honey and protect their young. Wasps do not make honey.

42

Weird!

Long ago, people thought the earth was flat. Some thought you could sail off the edge of the earth. Why can't you sail off the edge of the earth?

43

The earth is round, and gravity keeps everything on earth from escaping.

Look!

You can tell a lot about an animal by looking at its feet. What could you tell about an animal with webbed feet?

Animals with webbed feet spend a lot of time in water.

44

Really?

When you take a picture with a camera, you need to have light. Why do you need light?

The rays of sunlight interact with chemicals on the film that make the picture. This is why photographs must be developed in the dark or under special lights that do not affect the film. A digital camera does not have film, but it has a plate that is sensitive to light.

Fact!

Most plants have green leaves and need sunlight. What will happen if a plant does not get sunlight?

The plant turns yellow and brown because it needs the light to produce its green color.

46

Neat!

Magnets are fun. They are also useful. They can push and pull other magnets and certain metals. How do magnets push or pull?

The poles of a magnet attract (pull) or repel (push) other magnets and some metals, especially those containing iron. A magnet causes an invisible electrical current, called a magnetic field. It is this moving current that pushes or pulls the object.

Listen!

Animals are able to move around, which helps them protect themselves. Plants cannot protect themselves in this way. How do some plants protect themselves?

Plants such as cacti have sharp thorns. Trees have hard trunks covered with bark. Can you think of other ways plants protect themselves?

48

Really?

Plants cannot move from place to place as animals do. But plants do grow in new places over time. How can plants spread to new places?

The seeds of plants travel by wind, by water, and by being carried by animals.

science challenge

Level 1

Weird!

Most animals are very small when they are born. Opossums are so tiny that three babies would fit in a teaspoon! Where do baby opossums hide until they are big?

Opossums live in a pouch on their mother's body for a month. Then they cling to her back for another two until they are large enough to explore the world outside.

50

Who Knew?

Water falls from the clouds as rain, hail, or snow. How does water get into the clouds?

51

By evaporation. Water vapor in the air travels upward and condenses into clouds. When conditions are right, the water falls as rain or snow.

Cool!

On a hot day, the lifeguard at the pool where José swims sprays the walk around the pool with water. Why does he do this?

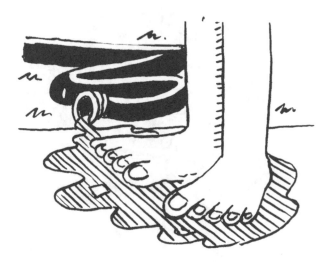

52

To cool the pavement. As the water evaporates, it absorbs heat energy and cools the pavement. This allows people to walk around the pool without burning their feet.

Fact!

Air pushes in on your body and on everything around you. What happens when air pushes in on an object?

53

If the pressure inside is the same, nothing happens. However, if the pressure inside is less, the object will be squeezed.

Fact!

We use energy every day, breathing, digesting food, and moving. Which uses the most energy: cleaning your room, watching TV, or riding your bike?

Riding your bike. The more large-muscle groups you use at once, and the harder you work, the more energy you use.

54

Weird!

Juanell stirred two spoons of salt into two spoons of hot water. Then she wrote a message in this invisible ink. In thirty minutes, the message disappeared. How could you read the message later?

55

The water will evaporate, but tiny bits of salt are left on the paper. If you rub the paper lightly with a pencil, the salty writing will appear.

Look!

Maple seeds have wings that make the seeds whirl as they fall. What causes the seeds to whirl? Why would this be an important feature in a seed?

The air flowing past the wings makes them whirl round and round. The wind can carry the seeds farther from the tree than if they just dropped to the ground. There is a better chance that some seeds will make it to good soil where they can grow.

56

Listen!

Honeybees can't talk, but they can tell other bees where to find flowers and nectar. How do they do this?

57

Honeybees talk to each other by dancing. A circular dance means that nectar is close by. A dance that follows a figure-8 pattern means the nectar is farther away.

Neat!

The moon looks like a giant orange pumpkin coming up behind the trees. But as it gets higher in the sky, it looks smaller. Why do you think the moon looks so large when it is rising?

58

One theory is that the rising moon looks larger because you see it behind trees and buildings and, in comparison, it looks larger.

Look!

Leaves have different shapes. You probably know what maple leaves look like. Look at other kinds of leaves. How could you show different shapes of leaves?

59

You can do two things. You can make leaf rubbings by placing a leaf wrong side up under a sheet of paper. With a crayon, rub gently over the paper. The shape of the leaf will appear. You can press fresh leaves by placing them in an old telephone book and letting them dry. Then mount them on paper and identify them. You can make a book!

Who Knew?

Elephants have been around for 58 million years. The first elephants were the size of pigs. They were only about three feet tall. How big was the biggest elephant that ever lived?

60

The largest of all elephants were the mammoths. The best known is the woolly mammoth. It was about eleven feet tall at the shoulder, and its tusks were about fifteen feet long. Mammoths became extinct about 10,000 years ago.

Cool!

The first space capsules were called Sputnik. There were eight of them. Sputnik I was launched in 1957 by the former Soviet Union. Who was the first American in space?

The first American astronaut was Alan Shepard, who was rocketed into space May 5, 1961.

Listen!

Animals can't talk, but they do communicate. If your cat purrs and rubs against you, it's happy to see you. What does it mean when your cat arches its back and spits?

Your cat is showing you that she's frightened or angry. Animals use body language and noise to tell what they feel.

62

Really?

Some insects, such as grasshoppers, shed their skins each time they grow larger. Why must grasshoppers shed their skins to grow?

OLD SKIN

63

Grasshoppers' skeletons are on the outside of their bodies. Because this exoskeleton is stiff and cannot stretch, it must be shed before the grasshopper can grow larger.

Weird!

Plants perspire just as you do in the summertime. Water vapor escapes through tiny holes in the leaves. How can you prove that plants perspire?

64

Place a glass jar or plastic bag over a potted plant in a sunny place. Do not add water to the plant. Check the inside surface of the container after an hour.

Who Knew?

The earth is always moving. It moves in two ways. It spins like a top and, as it spins, it circles around the sun. How can you tell that the earth is moving?

65

You can see how the sun seems to move from east to west. The earth is actually moving around the sun.

Listen!

A barometer is an instrument used to measure air pressure. Have you heard a meteorologist say, "The barometer is falling"? What does this mean?

It means that the air pressure is getting lower. This probably means that a storm is coming.

66

Look!

Mars is often called the "red planet." When Voyager landed on Mars, it sent back pictures proving the soil of Mars is red. If an astronaut on Mars looked at earth, what color would she see?

67

The planet earth would look blue because of its water and air. You can see this in the photos taken from the moon.

Listen!

Tyrone does not like to eat vegetables. But his mother says vegetables are good for him. Why should Tyrone eat his vegetables?

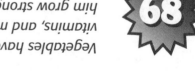

Vegetables have carbohydrates, vitamins, and minerals that help him grow strong.

68

Neat!

Rockets fly because of gases pushing them. The gases rush out of the back of the rocket. In what direction does the rocket move?

69

The rocket moves in the opposite direction of the gases. As most rockets are pointed upward, they move toward the sky.

Cool!

Some animals have special patterns of spots, stripes, or colors in their fur. How do these patterns help them survive?

Most animals do not see colors, only black, white, and gray. Spots, stripes, and colors help the animal blend into the background and hide from enemies.

70

Weird!

Everyone knows that most birds fly. But some animals "fly" too. Have you heard of flying foxes or flying squirrels? How do these animals "fly"?

71

Flying foxes are large bats that look a bit like foxes. They fly using their wings, just like other bats. Flying squirrels don't really fly. They use a wide flap of skin between their front and back legs to glide from tree to tree.

Fact!

You can bend your elbow, sit down, and wiggle your toes because you have joints. What is a joint?

A joint is any connection between two neighboring bones, together with the muscles or cartilage that allow it to move. See how many joints you can find in your body. (Don't forget your fingers and toes!)

72

Who Knew?

How is a goldfish like your bathroom?

73

They both have scales.

Really?

Most plants make their own food.
But some plants trap insects as well.
What plants trap insects?

Venus flytrap and pitcher plants both
trap insects. These plants grow in
bogs. The insects give them minerals
that they need to grow and can't get
from the acid water in the bogs.

74

Neat!

Michael shows Lateesha a trick. He sucks lemonade into his straw. Then he covers the top of the straw with his finger and pulls it out of the lemonade. What will happen?

The lemonade that is in the straw stays there. Air pushing up keeps it there. If Michael takes his finger off the straw, air pressure will act on the top, and the lemonade will drain out.

Cool!

Try this. Fill a bowl with water. Push the open end of a glass straight down into the water. Only a little water will go into the glass. What is keeping the water out?

There is air in the glass. The water pushes the air into the space at the top of the glass. Tilt the glass slightly to the side and see what happens.

76

Weird!

Electricity can attract water. Try combing your hair several times. Then hold your comb beside some running water. What happens?

By combing your hair, you have given your comb an electrical charge. The water is attracted and will bend toward the comb.

Fact!

Pints, liters, and quarts are ways that we measure fluids. What are some ways to measure distance?

Centimeters, meters, kilometers, inches, feet, and miles are measures of distance.

78

Listen!

The water in the ocean is salty. The water in (almost all) lakes is not salty and sometimes freezes in the winter. Will saltwater freeze?

79

Yes, but at much lower temperatures than freshwater.

Look!

Butterflies and moths look very much alike. But there are ways to tell them apart. How can you tell a moth from a butterfly?

Moths have feathery antennae and usually fly at night. Butterflies have knobbed antennae and fly during the day. When moths rest, they spread their wings flat. Butterflies keep their wings pointed up.

80

Really?

Turtles have been on earth for millions of years. Even long ago, turtles had shells much like the turtles you know. The biggest turtle that ever lived was Archelon. How big was Archelon?

81

Archelon was twelve feet long and eleven feet wide. This turtle lived in the ancient sea.

Fact!

Electricity is an important kind of energy. It makes the lights in your house glow. It runs the TV, the toaster, and many other things. When have you seen electricity in nature?

You have probably seen lightning in a thunderstorm. This is electricity that builds up in clouds.

82

Who Knew?

Some kinds of insects live together in groups. They have a queen and many workers. Bees are insects that live like this. What is another group that lives in a group?

83

Ants and termites live in groups, too.

Weird!

Some animals that look like insects are really not insects. An Li found something under a pile of leaves. It looked like a caterpillar, but it had many little legs. It moved very quickly. What was this animal?

It was a centipede. Centipedes are not worms or insects. They belong to a group of animals called chilopods (key-lo-pods). (Or it could have been a millipede, in the class diplopoda.)

84

Cool!

An air-filled bottle will float. Sometimes people put messages in bottles and throw them into the sea. It's fun to wait for someone to find the message. What happens if you add a little water to the bottle?

85

It will still float, but your message will get soggy! If you add too much water, the bottle will sink.

Listen!

Most birds are smaller than people. They need to be small and light so they can fly. What is the largest bird?

The African ostrich is the largest bird. It can be up to eight feet tall and weigh up to 345 pounds! Ostriches don't fly, but they can run up to forty miles per hour.

86

Fact!

Frogs and toads can live in water and on land. Both frogs and toads lay their eggs in water, where they hatch. What are animals that can live on both water and land called?

87

Animals that live on water and on land are called amphibians.

Weird!

Marco is petting his kitten's fur. Suddenly, he hears a crackling sound and feels a shock. His kitten's fur is standing straight up. What caused the crackling sound and the shock?

88

The crackling sound and the shock are caused by static electricity. When you shuffle across a carpet on a cool, dry day, you will pick up some electricity. If you reach out to a doorknob or other metal, you may get a shock.

Neat!

The largest plant in the world is the redwood tree. The tallest known redwood is the Mendocino tree in northern California. It is nearly 368 feet tall. What is the smallest plant in the world?

89

You may have seen the smallest plant in the world growing on a pond. It is called duckweed. Its flower is only $1/8$ of an inch wide.

Fact!

Do you have a Boston fern at your house? Ferns do not have flowers or seeds. How do ferns spread?

Ferns spread by spores. If you turn over a fern leaf, you may see little brown specs that look like seeds. Hold a paper under the leaf. Shake it gently. Do you see brown dust? These are spores that can grow new ferns.

Who Knew?

Cats and some other kinds of animals can see in the dark. How can they do this?

91

If you have a cat, look at the shape of its pupils. Your pupils are round but your cat's are oval. The cat's pupils can open wide at night to pick up more light. They can close to a slit in daylight to shut out bright light.

Neat!

Hot air rises. Long ago, someone thought of a way of using hot air to travel in the sky. How can people use hot air to travel above the earth?

92

Hot-air balloons lift passengers above the earth.

Really?

David's mom bought vegetables that looked like large green pinecones. She told him they were artichokes. When David eats an artichoke, what part of the plant will he be eating?

93

Artichokes are flower buds.

Really?

The largest seed in the world weighs up to forty-five pounds. It takes ten years to ripen. What is the largest seed in the world?

94

Who Knew?

Your heart will beat more than two billion times in your lifetime. What does your heart do to keep you healthy?

95

The heart pumps blood to all parts of your body. This carries food and oxygen to all of your cells.

Weird!

Angie tells Mark she can move a sheet of paper on the table without touching it. How can she do it? What moves the paper?

96

She blows on the paper. The moving air of her breath moves the paper.

Cool!

The sky looks blue. So do lakes and oceans. Have you ever wondered why? Fill a clear bottle with water and a few drops of milk. Darken the room. Shine a light through the bottle. What do you see?

White light has all the colors of the rainbow. But small particles, such as dust and milk drops, bend the color blue most, so this color shows more.

Look!

Plants need light like we need food. Plants use light to make food. What happens if you turn a plant away from a window it has been facing?

The plant will slowly turn its leaves to face the window and the light. This is called heliotropism.

98

Listen!

Water is important to all living things. We need to use water carefully. How can you use water carefully?

99

Do not waste water by letting the faucet run. Take short showers. Store water in the refrigerator to keep it cold (instead of running the faucet till the water is cold). Water your lawn in the afternoon or evening when there will not be as much evaporation.

Really?

Long ago people thought sickness was caused by evil spirits. Now we know that germs cause illness. How does your body fight diseases?

Your skin protects against some germs. So do white blood cells in your blood. Shots from your doctor can also prevent disease. Your body develops immunity when you receive a shot.

100

Neat!

You can make a musical instrument. Collect several sizes of rubber bands. Stretch them across a shoe box and strum them. What causes the rubber bands to make different sounds?

The rubber bands are of different thicknesses, lengths, and tensions. These differences make each band vibrate differently.

Fact!

Roots of plants are important. They help to hold the plant in the soil. What else do roots do?

They carry water and food from the soil into the plant.

102

Look!

Frogs and toads lay their eggs in water. The eggs have little black specks instead of yolks. They do not have shells. How can you tell if eggs you have found are frog's eggs or toad's eggs?

103

Frog's eggs are found in clumps or sheets. Toads lay their eggs in strings.

Cool!

Some birds do not fly. The penguin is one of these. Most penguins live near oceans and catch fish and squid. How do they catch fish?

Penguins' wings have turned into flippers. They use their flippers to swim fast and catch the fish and squid.

104

Neat!

The air around us has moisture in it. Fill a plastic cup with ice cubes. Pour water over the ice. Add a few drops of food coloring. Later check the outside of the cup. What has happened?

105

The cup looks as though it's sweating. You can tell the water did not leak out of the cup because it's clear, but you colored the cup's water. When warm air comes in contact with the cold cup, the moisture in the air condenses on the cup.

Listen!

Patrick was getting a checkup from his doctor. The doctor listened to Patrick's heart with a stethoscope. How does a stethoscope help the doctor listen?

THUMPA THUMPA THUMP

106

The stethoscope concentrates the sound. This helps the doctor clearly hear the sound waves the heart makes when it is pumping blood. It can also help the doctor hear the sound of your lungs breathing.

Fact!

Friction can be a problem in machines such as bicycles. Friction causes heat and wear on metal parts. What can you do to reduce friction?

107

You can make the parts that move against each other very slippery. Oil is slippery. That's why we add oil to the parts of a bike and the engine in a car.

Fact!

Animals such as lizards, toads, and snakes are called "cold-blooded." To get warm, they need a warm place. To cool off, they need a cool place. How do snakes survive in the desert?

They warm themselves in the morning sun. Then they find a cool burrow underground when the sun is hot.

108

Really?

Many people are afraid of bees and wasps because they sting. They forget that these insects are very important to people. How do bees and wasps help people?

109

These insects are important to us because they pollinate many plants. They move pollen from one flower to another. This allows the plant to make fruit and seeds. If bees and wasps did not pollinate plants, we would not have fruits and vegetables.

Who Knew?

Spiders live almost everywhere. Many of them spin webs that trap insects. Are spiders insects?

No, spiders are not insects. Count their legs. Spiders belong to a family called arachnids.

110

Neat!

Earthworms are important animals. Why? It's not because they are sometimes used for fish bait. How are earthworms important?

Earthworms help to enrich the soil. Also, by tunneling under the soil, they mix and loosen the soil. This lets air into the ground. The air is good for plant roots.

Really?

Some flowers bloom only at night. Often these flowers are light-colored or white. Night bloomers are sometimes fragrant. How do the colors and smells help these flowers?

112

The light colors are easier to see in the dark and the sweet smell is often stronger at night. Light colors and strong scents attract moths, other insects, and bats that pollinate the flowers.

Fact!

Wind can do work for us. Have you seen windmills? They are used for pumping water out of the ground and for grinding grain. How does wind power a windmill?

Moving air forces the blades of the windmill to turn.

Look!

Trees can live a long time. How long? Some oaks and maple trees can live to be 200 years old. How can you tell how old a tree is?

You can measure around the trunk. This will tell you about how old the tree is. If the tree has been cut down, you can count the rings on the stump. Trees grow a new ring every year.

114

Neat!

Warm air rises and cold air sinks. You can show this. Hold a balloon over a lighted lamp. Let it go. Does the balloon rise or sink?

115

The air over the lamp is warm. The balloon will rise with the warm air but will sink as soon as it drifts into cooler air.

Weird!

Jeremy says he is having roots, seeds, and berries for lunch! If he offers to share with you, what do you think you might have to eat?

Roots could be carrot sticks or potatoes; seeds could be peanuts or beans or rice; and berries could be strawberries, blueberries, or cranberries.

116

Cool!

Tony and Julio made a telephone.
They used string and paper cups.
How do paper cups and string carry
a message?

117

When you speak into the cup, it
vibrates with your voice. The cup
makes the string vibrate and it
carries the vibrations to the cup on
the other end. The string makes the
other cup vibrate, and you hear the
voice on the other end.

Fact!

Microbes are very tiny living things. Some cause disease. But others help to break down dead plants and animals. What would happen if microbes didn't break down dead materials?

The chemicals and nutrients in dead materials are used over and over again. If dead material did not break down, waste would pile up on the earth.

118

Neat!

Have you ever played on a seesaw? Seesaws are like a balance. You can move the seesaw or yourself to make it balance. How can you balance a seesaw if your friend is heavier than you?

119

You could change the center of gravity. You can do this by making your end of the seesaw longer and your friend's shorter. You could also ask another friend to sit with you. What might happen then?

Look!

Have you ever watched two kittens playing? One kitten may jump out at another. Sometimes they creep up on each other. This kind of play is very important. Why?

The kittens are learning how to protect themselves from larger animals. They are also learning skills that will help them catch mice!

120

Who Knew?

Grass is one of the most common plants in the world. It grows almost everywhere. There are many kinds of grass that are important foods for people! What kinds of grass are foods for people?

121

Rice, wheat, corn, and oats are all plants from the grass family. Think about this when you choose your breakfast cereal!

Fact!

Rocks and minerals are all around. They are used in many different ways. How can you tell a rock from a mineral?

Most minerals are made from one substance and many have crystals. Some of the minerals that you may see every day are things such as table salt, pencil lead (graphite), glass (silica), and diamonds. Rocks may have several minerals in them, depending on how they were formed.

122

Weird!

Mercury is the planet closest to the sun. A year on Mercury is eighty-eight days long. Would you be older or younger if you lived on Mercury?

123

You would be older if you lived on Mercury, because the years are shorter than they are on earth. Your birthday would come every eighty-eight days.

Neat!

James lives on a farm. He raises chickens and ducks. He also has a pet kitten and calf. The kitten and calf drink their mother's milk. What are animals that drink milk from their mothers called?

Animals that get milk from their mothers are called mammals.

124

Really?

There are several different kinds of kangaroos. The largest may weigh up to 200 pounds and be six feet tall. How small is the smallest kangaroo?

125

Musky rat kangaroos, which are the smallest kangaroos, are about one foot high and weigh about a pound.

Fact!

Do plants always grow from seeds? Some plants such as African violets, ivy, and coleus, are easier to grow from cuttings. How can you grow plants from cuttings?

Cuttings are pieces of a plant, such as an African violet leaf with its stalk, or a leafy stem from an ivy or coleus. Fill a small jar or glass half full with water, and drop the cutting in the jar. Roots will grow from the stem.

126

Weird!

People have always wished they could talk to animals. However, people have learned to talk to chimpanzees. How can people talk to chimpanzees?

127

People have used two kinds of language to talk to chimpanzees. Sign language (American Sign Language, or ASL) is the same language hearing-impaired people use. The other language is Yerkish. This is a language that uses a special computer keyboard. Chimpanzees can use the keyboard to talk to people.

Look!

Some kinds of sharks are very dangerous to other animals and sometimes people. Sharks do not have bones as other animals do. What do sharks have in place of bones?

Sharks have cartilage, which is like the tissue in your nose or your ear. But in sharks it is harder and stronger. It feels almost like bone.

128

Listen!

You can use a lever to do many kinds of work. A lever can help you lift or push something large. Which of these items is a lever: a pair of scissors, a hammer, or a wheelbarrow?

All of these things are levers! Levers have three parts. A fulcrum is the spot where the lever pivots. You push down or lift up to make the force. The load works in the opposite direction to the force.

129

science challenge

Level 1

Neat!

A praying mantis is a good helper to have in your garden. Some garden companies sell egg cases of the praying mantis. What makes the mantis so helpful?

The mantis eats many insect pests. Its big eyes help it spot caterpillars and beetles that could harm your garden. It is always hungry and has lots of babies that are also hungry!

130

Weird!

Nothing travels faster than light. Light can travel from the moon in 1.3 seconds. The distance to the moon averages 384,000 kilometers. If you could walk to the moon, how long would it take?

131

It would take about ten years to walk to the moon. The Apollo spaceships took three days to reach the moon.

Really?

Electricity is powerful energy. Did you know that some kinds of fish make electricity? Electric eels are one of these. How much electricity can an electric eel produce?

132

Electric eels can produce up to 650 volts of electricity. This is enough to stun a large animal.

Who Knew?

Almost all living things need sunlight to live. Deep in the ocean, there is no sunlight. Yet many animals live there. How do they live without sunlight?

133

There are minerals in the water that the fish, snails, and mussels can break down into food. In addition, some food falls down from the lighted zone above.

Fact!

There are many different climates in the world. Some people live in cold climates. Some live in hot climates. Most live in climates with seasons. What kind of climate do you live in?

You probably live in a temperate climate. Temperate climates are moderate in temperature and rainfall.

134

Cool!

Dragonflies have been on the earth for more than 300 million years! Their wings beat 1,600 times or more a minute—you can't see them move! They are great hunters. What do dragonflies hunt?

135

Dragonflies hunt mosquitoes and other small insects! They can bend their legs into a kind of basket shape. They swoop down and capture mosquitoes with this basket.

Who Knew?

Everyone knows that a red light means stop and a green light means go. Do you know why traffic lights are red and green and not blue and purple?

Red and green colors are easier for your eyes to see in poor light. Blue and purple are harder to tell apart and harder to see in dim light.

136

Weird!

Brad found a green tree toad. He put the toad into a box. When he opened the box, the green toad was gone. A gray toad was in the box! Where is the green toad?

The gray toad is the same toad as the green toad. Tree toads can change their colors to match what they are resting on.

Really?

Long ago, sailors believed that monsters lived in the sea. It is true that many large creatures live in oceans. What mammal is almost as large as a small whale?

The mammal is an elephant seal. It grows to be twenty feet long and may weigh as much as four tons. Elephant seals do not live in the water all the time.

138

Listen!

Many animals sing. They always sing the same song over and over. What animal changes its song from year to year?

Scoo...bee..
doo..bee.doo

139

Weird!

As you grow, your bones get longer and your skin gets larger. Animals such as snakes grow differently. When they grow, they burst out of their skins. Why do snakes grow in this way?

The outer covering of a snake's body is always being worn by friction as it crawls and doesn't stretch or grow the way your skin does. When a snake sheds its skin, it even sheds the part that covers its eyes!

140

Listen!

Weather is important to people. Sunshine and rain are important for growing food. Some things we do are harmful to weather. What is smog?

141

Smog is smoke and fumes that mix with moisture in the air. You can see smog. It looks like a dirty brown cloud.

Fact!

Not all butterflies hatch from cocoons. Some butterflies, such as monarchs, hatch from a pupa. What is the difference between a cocoon and a pupa?

A pupa is the insect, a cocoon is a covering made by the insect. Cocoons are usually made from materials such as leaves or tiny twigs and silk from the insect's body. Cocoons protect pupas from harm and the weather. Some pupas spend the winter in a cocoon. When a butterfly hatches directly from a pupa, it is like shedding the skin.

142

Cool!

Cody and Thomas were playing with toy cars. They built a ramp and raced the cars down it. What force made the cars roll down the ramp?

143

The cars rolled down the ramp because of gravity.

Look!

Once people believed that the sun and all the planets traveled around the earth. How did they find out the sun was at the center?

They observed the motions of the planets. They realized that it was hard to explain these movements. The only way the movements made sense was if the sun was in the center and did not move.

144

Really?

If you have ever seen pictures of a shark, you probably remember its long, sharp teeth. Sharks' teeth are unusual. How are sharks' teeth different from other animals' teeth?

145

Sharks' teeth are arranged in many rows. If they lose one, a new tooth from another row moves into its place.

Who Knew?

Whistling tea kettles tell you when the water in the kettle is boiling. What makes the tea kettle whistle?

146

Most tea kettles that whistle do so because hot water expands and produces steam. The steam expands and pushes air and steam through the whistle, making the sound.

Fact!

Birds and many reptiles lay eggs. Most birds build nests, but reptiles often dig holes in the soil for their eggs. How are reptiles' eggs kept warm?

147

The soil is warmed by the sun. Some alligators pile decaying plants over the eggs they lay. Heat from the plants warms the eggs.

Fact!

The earth and all the plants travel around the sun. Does the moon travel around the sun, too?

Yes. The moon orbits (circles around) the earth. But the earth and the moon together orbit the sun. Some of the other planets have moons that also orbit their planets. The planets and their moons orbit the sun together.

Neat!

Silk is a very beautiful fabric. It is called a natural fiber because its thread is not made by humans. How is silk made?

149

Silk comes from fibers spun by silkworms, an insect larva. Each silkworm makes one long fiber when it makes its cocoon. Each thread can be about 915 meters (1,000 yards) long.

Look!

A green plant will grow toward light. You can see this for yourself. Cut a window in a cardboard box. Plant some radish seeds in a pot and cover it with the box. What happens?

The plants bend toward the light. The cells on the dark side of the plant grow longer than those on the light side. This makes the plant grow toward light. This property is called heliotropism.

150

Who Knew?

Fireflies are sometimes called lightning bugs. But they aren't flies or bugs. What are they?

Fireflies are actually a kind of beetle. They use their flashing lights to attract mates.

Look!

If you watch the night sky, you may see a falling star. Do stars really fall out of the sky?

What looks like a falling star is probably a piece of rock from outer space called a meteor. When meteors enter earth's atmosphere, they are travelling very fast. They get so hot that they glow! Most of them burn up before they reach the ground.

152

Really?

Many animals have spots and stripes in their fur. Some insects look just like leaves or sticks. How does this camouflage help living things survive?

153

Spots and stripes help animals hide from enemies. Most animals do not see color, and these patterns help the animal hide against a background of leaves and trunks. Looking like a leaf or a twig helps insects to escape being noticed by hungry birds and animals!

Neat!

Jamal went fishing and fell into the creek. His father laid Jamal's wet clothes on a bush. Thirty minutes later they were dry. What happened to the water?

154

It evaporated. When water evaporates, it goes into the air.

Cool!

At the North and South Poles of the earth, there is always snow and ice—even in the summertime. Why does the snow never melt at the poles?

155

Even in the summer, the sun's rays are too weak to raise the temperature enough to melt the snow. For many months of the year, sunlight doesn't even reach the poles!

Fact!

Long ago, people found that water could help do hard work. Fast-moving rivers were good places to build factories. How did water help do work?

156

Water can make large wheels turn. The turning wheels make machinery move. In the past some of the machines would grind wheat or corn for flour. Some machines helped to spin thread and weave cloth. Some helped saw wood into lumber. We use water power today to make electricity.

Listen!

Your ears tell you a lot about the world around you. You can sometimes tell what is going on just by hearing sounds. Have a friend make a sound. Can you guess what the sound was?

157

You can do this without a friend, too. Just sit quietly in your house and listen.

Fact!

Some kinds of insects live together. Bees, ants, wasps, and termites live in groups. Many of these insects build homes. What materials do wasps use for their homes?

158

Some wasps use mud to build cells for their eggs. Other wasps build homes of paper. They make the paper from bits of chewed leaves, rotting wood, and plant stems.

Cool!

Dolphins are amazing animals. They seem to talk to each other. Dolphins have even learned to help people. How have dolphins helped people?

Dolphins communicate with each other using special sounds. For example, certain sounds mean danger and others are cries for help. Trained dolphins have learned that whistles can carry messages. They have helped divers locate objects underwater.

Weird!

Animals and insects do not see the way that people do. Their eyes are different from ours. Grasshoppers have five eyes! How are insects' eyes different from people's eyes?

Many insects such as grasshoppers have more than two eyes. They also have eyes with many lenses. What an insect sees probably looks like a picture made of many little pieces. Eyes like this are good at detecting motion and help protect the insect from being caught and eaten!

Who Knew?

Have you lost some of your baby teeth? New teeth grow in their place. Teeth are needed for chewing and talking. You have four kinds of teeth. What are the four kinds of teeth?

161

Molars and premolars (bicuspids), at the back of your mouth, grind food. Your front teeth, canines and incisors, are for biting and cutting food.

Look!

Have you ever seen a volcano erupting? Melted rock and steam pour out of it. Ashes make the sky dark. What is melted rock from a volcano called?

Melted rock is called magma when it is underground. Magma that reaches the surface is called lava. Lava flows down the sides of the volcano.

Cool!

Lynn and Zack went sledding. Later the sun melted the snow a bit. The next day their sleds went very fast. Why did their sleds go faster?

163

The sun had melted the snow a little. When it got cold at night, the melted snow turned to ice. Ice has less friction than snow, so the sleds went faster.

Fact!

Bones are different for different animals. The bones of a hummingbird are not like the bones of an elephant. Why are hummingbird bones different than elephant bones?

Hummingbirds don't need big, heavy bones. Their bones need to be light, strong, and tiny so they can fly easily. Bones of a heavy animal like an elephant are thick and solid while a hummingbird's bones are thin and hollow.

164

Neat!

Peter and Emalee made a sand castle by mixing sand and water together and forming towers and walls. Later, the sand castle fell apart. What happened that made the castle fall?

165

The water held the sand together in the shapes of towers and walls. When the water evaporated, the sand collapsed.

Really?

An octopus is an animal that lives in the sea. It has long arms and many suckers on each arm. The suckers help the octopus catch its food. How many arms does an octopus have?

166

The octopus has eight arms. (Octo means eight.) If one arm is chopped off, it will grow a new arm.

Who Knew?

Molds are organisms that grow from spores. You may have seen a green mold growing on bread or fruit. What important medicine comes from mold?

The medicine is penicillin. It was discovered by Dr. Alexander Fleming in 1928. Penicillin kills many dangerous bacteria that cause illness.

Fact!

Most plants need soil to grow. But many plants can be grown without soil. How can you grow plants without soil?

They can be grown in water-soaked sand or gravel or in water alone. This is called hydroponics. Some kinds of vegetables, such as tomatoes and lettuce, are grown this way. Plant food mixed in the water helps them grow big and strong.

Look!

Animals that hunt other animals for food are called predators. Predators have eyes on the front of their faces. Most prey animals have eyes on the sides of their faces. Is a rabbit a predator?

169

No. Rabbits have eyes on the sides of their faces. They need to be able to watch in two directions for their enemies, because they are prey.

Neat!

Your tongue has two different senses. You can taste sweet, sour, salty, and bitter things with your tongue. What other sense does your tongue have?

Your tongue has a sense of touch.

170

Look!

Long ago people used the sun and shadows to tell time. Morning shadows face west. Afternoon shadows face east. What time is it when there are no shadows?

171

Noon. At midday the sun is directly overhead.

Listen!

People sing because they are happy. But birds sing for a different reason. What is the reason that birds sing?

Birds sing to attract mates. They also sing to warn other birds to stay away. When they sing, they are saying, "This is my area. The space here belongs to me." This space is called the bird's territory.

172

Weird!

Some plants and insects depend on each other. The yucca plant and the yucca moth do. How do yucca plants and yucca moths depend on each other?

173

The yucca moth pollinates the flowers of the yucca plant. The yucca plant produces seeds that the yucca moth caterpillars eat. There are many seeds and some are left uneaten and grow into new yucca plants.

Who Knew?

Pinecones can tell you whether the air is damp or dry. How do they do this?

When the air is damp, the cones will close up tight. When it is dry, they open wide. They do this because the seeds can travel farther when it is dry.

174

Really?

The picture on a color television is made up of tiny dots. The dots are only three colors—red, blue, and green. What makes the other colors?

175

The other colors are combinations of these three colors along with white. The dots that are combined are too small to be seen and your eyes and brain are fooled into believing that they see the other colors!

Look!

Have you ever watched a turtle eat? The mouths of turtles are different from most other animals. How are turtles' mouths different?

176

Turtles do not have lips or teeth! Instead, their jaws have sharp edges and are shaped like beaks. They are able to bite off bits of grass and leaves, or tear apart small fish, with this sharp beak. Turtles do have tongues, which help them to swallow.

Really?

If you have a fish tank, one thing that you need to do is place plants in the tank. Why should you do this?

177

Plants give off oxygen. Fish need oxygen to breathe. Even though there is oxygen in the water, it is good to increase the oxygen supply. Plants also provide a place for fish to hide.

Weird!

Darnell was digging in his garden. He accidentally dug into an earthworm and chopped it in two.

His dad said the worm would still live. Can an earthworm live if it is chopped in two?

Yes, earthworms can live if they are chopped in two. They have a nervous system that is spread along the length of the body. The nervous system takes the place of a brain. Earthworms can grow new parts if less than half of the body is lost.

178

Who Knew?

Natural sponges come from deep in the ocean. For many years, people thought sponges were a kind of plant. Now we know this isn't so. What are sponges?

Sponges are actually animals. They have no legs, fins, or stomachs. Sponges get food by pumping water through small openings in their bodies. Natural sponges that you buy are the skeletons of these animals.

Level 1

Neat!

Leaves are green because of the chlorophyll inside them. But in the fall, leaves change colors. What makes leaves change colors in the fall?

In the fall, the leaf produces less and less chlorophyll as the days get shorter. The green chlorophyll disappears, and other colors in the leaf that were covered by the green appear.

180

Who Knew?

On Jupiter things weigh almost three times as much as they do on earth. On Mars, things weigh only half of what they weigh here. On which planet is gravity strongest? Why?

On Jupiter because it has a larger mass.

Really?

The Saharan desert gets 4,300 hours of sun a year—it's the sunniest place on earth. How many days of sun is that? How much rain does the Sahara get a year?

About 179 days, almost half a year.
About three inches a year, mostly
from December to March.

182

Listen!

Most garbage from American cities ends up in landfills. What is a landfill?
What are some of the problems with landfills?

183

A landfill is a plastic-lined pit. Garbage is dumped there until the landfill is full. Garbage does not decay in a landfill, so we need to find new landfills whenever one fills up. Dangerous chemicals from the garbage can leak into the soil and water. No buildings can be built on an old landfill, and the land can't be used for farming.

Listen!

What are some ways that we could throw less garbage into landfills?

We can use fewer things that make garbage. We can recycle many things, like paper or aluminum cans. We can compost yard waste.

Cool!

In 2004 NASA launched the Mars Rovers. These dune buggy-like vehicles drove over Mars and found signs of water. Why was this an important discovery?

All life we know on earth needs water to live. If there was once water on Mars, there may also have been life.

Look!

In the night sky, we can see stars, the moon, and planets. But once in a while, we can see something different, called a comet. What is a comet?

A comet is a big chunk of rock and ice. As it orbits (circles) the sun, some of the rock and ice is pulled off and burns. Thus, the comet glows and often seems to have a long tail.

186

Fact!

Animals can be divided into three groups, based on the kinds of foods they eat. What are these three groups?

Herbivores (like deer) eat only plants. Carnivores (like wolves) eat only meat. Omnivores (like people) eat a mixture of plants and meat.

Who Knew?

Put some ice cubes in a pan and heat it on the stove. Watch the ice cubes melt and the water begin to boil. You have just seen the three states of matter. What are they?

Everything in the universe is a solid (like ice), a liquid (like water), or a gas (like steam).

Fact!

What is a natural resource? Can you name some? Why is it important to use natural resources wisely?

189

A natural resource is anything of value that comes from the earth. Examples are oil, wood, water, or gold. If we use up a natural resource, we have no way to make more.

Who Knew?

Why does lightning always come before thunder? How can you use thunder to tell how far away a thunderstorm is?

Lightning and thunder really happen at the same time. But light travels faster than sound. So we see the flash before we hear the boom. Count the seconds between the lightning and the thunder. Each five seconds equals one mile away.

190

Really?

What is the biggest living lizard on earth? How big can it get? How long can it live?

The Komodo dragon of Indonesia is the biggest lizard. It can reach 10 feet in length, weigh 300 pounds, and live 100 years. Sometimes Komodo dragons even attack humans.

191

Weird!

Most lakes contain freshwater. But some are salty. Can you name some? Why are they salty?

192

The Great Salt Lake, the Dead Sea, and the Caspian Sea are salty. Freshwater picks up a little salt as it flows over the land. These lakes are landlocked—water flows in, but there is no way for it to flow out. As water evaporates from the lake, it leaves the salt behind.